D1600725

# THEODORE ROOSEVELT'S WORDS OF WIT AND WISDOM

# THEODORE ROOSEVELT'S
# WORDS OF WIT
# AND WISDOM

**CHARTWELL
BOOKS**

## CHARTWELL
## BOOKS

an imprint of Book Sales
a division of Quarto Publishing Group USA Inc.
142 West 36th Street, 4th Floor
New York, New York 10018

CHARTWELL BOOKS and the distinctive
Chartwell Books logo are trademarks of
Quarto Publishing Group USA Inc.

ISBN-13: 978-0-7858-3394-9

Printed in China

2 4 6 8 10 9 7 5 3 1

www.quartous.com

# Contents

THERE HAS NEVER YET BEEN A MAN IN OUR HISTORY WHO LED A LIFE OF EASE WHOSE NAME IS WORTH REMEMBERING.

# THEODORE ROOSEVELT

THEODORE ROOSEVELT WAS BORN IN NEW YORK City, October 27, 1858. On his father's side he is from Dutch emigrant stock, and most of his ancestors have been successful merchants prominent in the commercial life of New York. His grandfather was an explorer of the Ohio and Mississippi Rivers on the first steamboat that navigated them. His mother, Martha Bullock, was from the South, born near Atlanta, Ga., and from which place she married the President's father, Theodore Roosevelt, in 1853.

Roosevelt began his preparation for college in the autumn of 1873, when fourteen years of age, under the direction of Mr. Arthur H. Cutler, of the Cutler School, New York City. This was after the return from a long trip in Europe and Egypt. His health was not good, but Mr. Cutler, in a letter to the present writer, says that while at school he then showed "the alert mind, retentive memory, and earnestness of purpose which has since marked his public life and his private life." He entered Harvard University in 1876, graduating in 1880, and prepared for the bar at Columbia University.

He was elected to the legislature of New York in 1882, in which he served three terms, and it is said that during that time he introduced and carried through more important city legislation than was ever brought about by any one preceding him.

In 1884, through domestic troubles and ill health, Roosevelt abandoned his political work in New York and went to North Dakota, where he had purchased a cattle-ranch of considerable size. Here the continued out-of-door life brought him health and strength.

In 1886 he returned to the East as a candidate for mayor of New York, but failed to secure election. The next three years were devoted almost entirely to literary and historical work.

In 1889 Roosevelt was appointed a member of the Civil Service Commission at Washington, and soon became its president, retaining that office until the spring of 1895. He had always been greatly interested in civil service reform, and during his connection with the commission the civil service rules were extended to more than

50,000 government employees, who before were not protected by them.

When W. L. Strong was elected mayor of New York in 1894, Roosevelt accepted under him the head of the police department, although many of his friends in Washington urged him not to, saying that it was beneath his dignity. During the two years that he held this office, however, he placed the police department on a new and thoroughly efficient basis, and successfully broke up the system of blackmail which had prevailed so extensively in the department, and likewise gained the admiration and good will of all members of the New York police force.

In 1897 President McKinley offered Roosevelt the position of Assistant Secretary of the Navy. The following year he resigned this position to become the lieutenant-colonel of the First U. S. Volunteer Cavalry, popularly known as the "Rough Riders." It had been through his efforts that the regiment had been formed, consisting largely of men recruited from the Southern and Western ranches, though among the volunteers were many college men. Dr. Leonard Wood, a friend of Roosevelt's, an army surgeon who had large experience in Indian fighting in Arizona, was made colonel, though shortly after the regiment's arrival in Cuba Wood was promoted to brigadier-general, and Roosevelt assumed command of the regiment as colonel.

On September 27, 1898, Roosevelt was nominated as governor of New York, and was elected by 20,000 majority. During his two years as governor he put through, among other important bills, a new civil service law, and the revision of the tenement-house laws.

He refused a second term as governor of New York to accept the nomination of Vice-President in McKinley's second term. On the assassination of McKinley in September, 1901, he assumed the duties of President of the United States.

Besides his arduous duties as a politician he has found much time to write, and several of his books are cited as authorities, noteworthily his "History of the Naval War of 1812," published in 1882. His other works are: "Winning of the West," 1889-96; "Hunting Trips of a Ranchman," 1885; "Life of Thomas Hart Benton," 1886; "Life of Gouverneur Morris," 1887; "Ranch Life and Hunting Trail," 1888; "History of New York," 1890; "American Ideals and Other Essays," 1897; "The Wilderness Hunter," 1893; "The Rough Riders," 1899; "Life of Oliver Cromwell," 1900; "The Strenuous Life," 1900, and part author of "The Deer Family," 1902.

Hereto are attached two estimates of Roosevelt by personal friends, though in different stations of life. The first by Jacob A. Riis, and the second by Bill Sewall, a guide in Maine, who also was his foreman on the ranch in North Dakota.

"A man with red blood in his veins, a healthy patriot with no clap-trap jingoism about him, but a rugged belief in America and its mission, an intense lover of country and flag, a vigorous optimist and believer in men, who looks for the good in them and finds it. Practical in partisanship, loyal, trusting, and gentle as a friend, unselfish, modest as a woman, clean-handed and clean-hearted, and honest to the core. In the splendid vigour of his young manhood he is the knightliest figure in American politics today, the fittest exponent of his country's idea, and the model for its young sons who are coming to take up the task he set them. For their sake I am willing to give him up and set him where they can all see him and strive to be like him. So we shall have little need of bothering about boss rule and misrule hereafter. We shall farm out the job of running the machine no longer; we shall be able to run it ourselves."—JACOB A. RIIS, *in the Review of Reviews.*

"If you want to ask me anything about Colonel Roosevelt, you can just go ahead, for I am never tired of praising him—my best friend, and the truest friend a man ever had. Roosevelt is, first of all, an honest man, and one of the plainest men I ever met. He doesn't judge a man by the clothes he wears, or by his position in life. He takes a man at his true worth, and he's been so ever since I can remember, which was when I met him here, as a boy, twenty-five years ago.

"No wonder his Rough Riders worshipped him. I'm no hero-worshipper myself, but I take off my hat to Colonel Roosevelt, the best and truest man I ever met. I know him, for I have eaten with him, and slept under the same blanket with him. They say that to know much about a man you must know him in that way.

"He'll never be a wealthy man. Why, I've known him to financially aid his political opponents when they got into a tight place, and he often told me that the only pleasure he got from money was in the good that he could do with it. He was always looking around for a chance to help some poor, worthy fellow.

"He hates sham and hypocrisy, and when he was a boy, hunting up here, he used to pick out the good, square fellows to chum with, no matter how they dressed or what their financial condition might be.

"I always said that he'd be President some day. I told him when he was only eighteen years old that he'd sit in the White House some day. Something told me that he would, and you see it has turned out true. He used to laugh at me. He never wanted to be in public life, then.

"Why, he wanted to be a naturalist. He loved to study trees and animals, and expected to devote his life to that sort of thing. One day, when we were out hunting, he said to me in a sober way:

"'Bill, I've been thinking about what I shall do in life, and I feel that if I were to follow my natural bent and be a naturalist I would be robbing my fellow men of more useful service. Consequently I have decided, much against my natural inclination, to go into public life, and for that I shall fit myself by study and training.'

"I am confident of one thing, and that is that unless some of those tricksters get him tangled up, they will never be able to get the better of him, and they will find him the hardest man to corrupt that they ever tackled. I know this as well as I know that I'm alive; I know his every trait, for I spent the happiest years of my life with him, both here and on his ranch in Dakota, where for three years I was his foreman.

"How did I come to meet Roosevelt? Well, it must be some twenty-five odd years ago that his cousins, Dr. J. West Roosevelt and W. E. Roosevelt, the latter a wealthy banker of New York, used to come here to hunt in the fall. Once they told me that they were going to invite a young relative of theirs up here.

"They said his name was 'Teddy' Roosevelt, and that he was a college student. They cautioned me about him, as I now recollect, saying that he was a gritty, headstrong youngster who had more sand in his crop than he had strength, and they wanted me to take the best of care of him.

"Well, he came. He was a pale, rather delicate young man of about eighteen, but the toughest boy physically and the greatest mentally that I ever met. I gave him the room right over this one we're sitting in, and we went out hunting. He took the greatest interest in the woods, and never complained of being tired, although I knew many a time that he was hardly able to drag himself home after a long tramp.

"That boy would never give up. He'd always take the biggest end of the stick, too, and many a time I was afraid he'd collapse on me, but he would cheer right up, and say he was as fresh as a daisy. Talk about grit! He was all grit.

"He came year after year, and we went out into the woods. Among others he met Bill Dow, the fairest and squarest man that ever lived, and the best shot in Aroostook County. That's Bill's picture over there on the wall. When he died I lost a good friend. We were together on Roosevelt's ranch out in the Bad Lands, and it was a toss-up who was foreman—Bill or myself. When Roosevelt started out on his new career, he didn't forget us, and asked Bill and me to go out to his ranch in Dakota.

"This was along in '84, and Bill and I went to New York to meet him. We found him in the Fifth

Avenue Hotel, surrounded by politicians, and when he spied us he rushed up with both hands held out. He was glad to see us, for a fact. Well, he engaged us to go out to Dakota. Neither of us knew anything about ranches or bucking bron-chos, but Colonel Roosevelt said that we were all right, and that he wanted some Maine men to look out for his interests.

"The ranch was located on the Little Missouri, about thirty miles from Medora, on the North-ern Pacific. Medora was named after the wife of the Marquis de Mores, and the marquis owned the lands on both sides of the Roosevelt ranch. He had in his employ the toughest lot of cowboys in that part of the country, and there was trouble in the air all the time. The marquis and his gang seemed to think they could run the whole coun-try, and threw a lot of big bluffs our way.

"Two men named Reilly and O'Donnell were told by the marquis that they were encroaching on his land, and notified by him that if they didn't get out at once they would be shot on sight. One day these two men were fired upon from ambush, Reilly being killed and O'Donnell crippled for life. The marquis was arrested and tried for the murder of Reilly, but his money saved him from the gallows—he was acquitted.

"Soon after this Bill and I were notified that if we didn't get East where we belonged our bones would be found on the ranch, and the life of Colonel Roosevelt also was threatened. The De Mores crowd claimed that we were on their land.

"A man named Paddock was De Mores' right-hand man, and he made the open threat that he would shoot Colonel Roosevelt on sight.

"The colonel was in New York at the time, but the day he got back to the ranch and heard what had been going on, he mounted his horse and rode straight over to the Do Mores ranch. He hunted up Paddock, and said:

"'I understand that you have threatened to kill me on sight. Now, I have come over to see when you want to begin the killing, and to inform you that if you have anything to say against me now is the time to say it.'

"Paddock turned pale, and stuttered out something about it being all a mistake; that he had never made any such threats. He made all sorts of apologies, and then Colonel Roosevelt rode back to his ranch.

"Next came a challenge from the Marquis de Mores to Colonel Roosevelt. The marquis sent a letter saying that the colonel had influenced one of the witnesses against him in the murder trial, and declaring that between gentlemen such differences could be settled in but one way, meaning, of course, by a duel. Colonel Roosevelt said to me:

"'Bill, I don't want to disgrace my family by fighting a duel; but I won't be bullied by a Frenchman. Now, as I am the challenged party, I have the privilege of naming the weapons. I am no swordsman, and pistols are too uncertain and Frenchy for me; so what do you say if I make it rifles?

"'I'll just write to the marquis, saying that I have not done anything to injure him, but if his letter is meant as a challenge, and he insists upon having satisfaction, I will meet him with rifles at ten paces—both to fire until one drops.'

"I was horrified, and said that such a fight meant certain death for one or both, but I couldn't stop it, and the colonel sat down on a log and wrote to De Mores, stating his terms of duelling. It must have frightened the marquis half to death, for the answer came by the very next post, to the effect that he had no intention of challenging Roosevelt—that what he meant by his letter was that 'differences between gentlemen could be settled without trouble.'

"The marquis and his wife came over to our ranch the next day and called upon Colonel Roosevelt, and always after that were very friendly.

"I don't think Roosevelt ever made a dollar out there, but, as I have said, he didn't care much for money. He seemed to enjoy the ranch life, and the cowboys thought a lot of him. He was a pretty good shot for a man who couldn't see a

XX ❧ THEODORE ROOSEVELT'S

foot without glasses, and we had a good many hunting trips together.

"After three years of ranching we decided to come back East. Roosevelt was being constantly called to New York, and had very little time to devote to the cattle business, anyway.

"I expect to see him soon, now, and I know he'll be just the same—he is the same Teddy Roosevelt, whether sitting in the White House, rounding up cattle in the Bad Lands, or hunting deer on the Aroostook River."—BILL SEWALL, *in the Boston Globe, Aug. 28, 1902.*

From his writings and speeches Roosevelt, the Man, shows predominantly, and we trust the readers of this little book will find enjoyment in his terse, epigrammatic thoughts.

# THEODORE ROOSEVELT'S
## WORDS OF WIT
## AND WISDOM

# Speech On William McKinley

*Delivered at Canton, Ohio, January 27, 1903.*

It was given to President McKinley to take the foremost place in our political life at a time when our country was brought face to face with problems more momentous than any whose solution we have ever attempted, save only in the Revolution and in the Civil War; and it was under his leadership that the nation solved these mighty problems aright. Therefore, he shall stand in the eyes of history, not merely as the first man of his generation, but as among the greatest figures in our national life, coming second only to the men of the two great crises in which the Union was founded and preserved.

No man could carry through, successfully, such a task as President McKinley undertook,

unless trained by long years of effort for its performance. Knowledge of his fellow citizens, ability to
understand them, keen sympathy with even their
innermost feelings, and yet power to lead them,
together with far-sighted sagacity and resolute
belief both in the people and in their future—all
these were needed in the man who headed the
march of our people during the eventful years
from 1896 to 1901. These were the qualities possessed by McKinley and developed by him
throughout his whole history previous to assum-
ing the presidency.

As a lad he had the inestimable privilege of
serving, first in the ranks, and then as a commis-
sioned officer, in the great war for National
Union, righteousness and grandeur; he was one
of those whom a kindly Providence permitted to
take part in a struggle which ennobled every man
who fought therein. He who when little more
than a boy had seen the grim steadfastness which
after four years of giant struggle restored the
Union and freed the slave, was not thereafter to
be daunted by danger or frightened out of his
belief in the great destiny of our people.

President McKinley's rise to greatness had in
it nothing of the sudden, nothing of the unex-
pected or seemingly accidental. Throughout his
long term of service in Congress there was a
steady increase alike in his power of leadership

and in the recognition of that power both by his associates in public life and by the public itself. Session after session his influence in the House grew greater; his party antagonists grew to look upon him with constantly increasing respect; his party friends with constantly increasing faith and admiration.

Eight years before he was nominated for President he was already considered a presidential possibility. Four years before he was nominated only his own high sense of honour prevented his being made a formidable competitor of the chief upon whom the choice of the convention then actually fell. In 1896 he was chosen because the great mass of his party knew him and believed in him and regarded him as symbolizing their ideals, as representing their aspirations.

But even as a candidate President McKinley was far more than the candidate of a party, and as President he was in the broadest and fullest sense the President of all the people of all sections of the country.

His first nomination came to him because of the qualities he had shown in healthy and open political leadership, the leadership which by word and deed impresses itself as a virile force for good upon the people at large, and which has nothing in common with mere intrigue or manipulation. But in 1896 the issue was fairly joined, chiefly

upon a question which as a party question was
entirely new, so that the old lines of political cleav-
age were in large part abandoned. All other issues
sank in importance when compared with the vital
need of keeping our financial system on the high
and honourable plane imperatively demanded by
our position as a great civilized power.

As the champion of such a principle President
McKinley received the support not only of his own
party but of hundreds of thousands of those to
whom he had been politically opposed. He tri-
umphed, and he made good with scrupulous
fidelity the promises upon which the campaign
was won. We were at the time in a period of great
industrial depression, and it was promised for and
on behalf of McKinley that if he were elected our
financial system should not only be preserved
unharmed, but improved and our economic system shaped in accordance with those theories
which have always marked our periods of greatest
prosperity. The promises were kept, and following their keeping came the prosperity which we
now enjoy. All that was foretold concerning the
well-being which would follow the election of
McKinley has been justified by the event.

But as so often happens in our history, the
President was forced to face questions other than
those at issue at the time of his election. Within a
year the situation in Cuba had become literally

intolerable. President McKinley had fought too well in his youth, he knew too well at first hand what war really was, lightly to enter into a struggle. He sought by every honourable means to preserve peace, to avert war. Then, when it became evident that these efforts were useless, that peace could not be honourably entertained, he devoted his strength to making the war as short and as decisive as possible. It is needless to tell the result in detail.

There followed a harder task. As a result of the war we came into possession of Cuba, Porto Rico, and the Philippines. In each island the conditions were such that we had to face problems entirely new to our national experience, and, moreover, in each island or group of islands the problems differed radically from those presented in the others. In Porto Rico the task was simple. The island could not be independent. It became in all essentials a part of the Union. It has been given all the benefits of our economic and financial system. Its inhabitants have been given the highest individual liberty, while yet their government has been kept under the supervision of officials so well chosen that the island can be appealed to as affording a model for all such experiments in the future.

In Cuba, where we were pledged to give the island independence, the pledge was kept not merely in letter but in spirit. It would have been a betrayal of our duty to have given Cuba independence out of hand. President McKinley, with his usual singular sagacity in the choice of agents, selected in General Leonard Wood the man of all others best fit to bring the island through its uncertain period of preparation for independence, and the result of his wisdom was shown when last May the island became in name and in fact a free republic, for it started with a better equipment and under more favourable conditions than had ever previously been the case with any Spanish-American commonwealth.

Finally, in the Philippines, the problem was one of great complexity. There was an insurrectionary party claiming to represent the people of the islands and putting forth their claims with a certain speciousness which deceived no small number of excellent men here at home, and which afforded to yet others a chance to arouse a factious party spirit against the President.

A weaker and less far-sighted man than President McKinley would have shrunk from a task very difficult in itself, and certain to furnish occasion for attack and misrepresentation no less than for honest misunderstanding. But President McKinley never flinched. He refused to consider the thought of abandoning our duty in our new possessions. While sedulously endeavouring to act with the utmost humanity toward the insurrectionists, he never faltered in the determination to put them down by force of arms, alike for the sake of our own interest and honour, and for the sake of the interest of the islanders, and particularly of the great numbers of friendly natives, including those most highly civilized, for whom abandonment by us would have meant ruin and death. Again his policy was most amply vindicated.

Peace has come to the islands, together with a greater measure of individual liberty and self-government than they have ever before known. All the tasks set us as a result of the war with Spain have so far been well and honourably accomplished, and as a result this nation stands higher than ever before among the nations of mankind.

President McKinley's second campaign was fought mainly on the issue of approving what he had done in his first administration, and specifically what he had done as regards these problems springing out of the war with Spain. The result was that the popular verdict in his favour was more overwhelming than it had been before.

We are gathered together tonight to recall his memory, to pay our tribute of respect to the great chief and leader who fell in the harness, who was stricken down while his eyes were bright with the "light that tells of triumph tasted." We can honour him best by the way we show in actual deed that we have taken to heart the lessons of his life. We must strive to achieve, each in the measure that he can, something of the qualities which made President McKinley a leader of men, a mighty power for good—his strength, his courage, his courtesy and dignity, his sense of justice, his ever present kindness and regard for the rights of others. He won greatness by meeting and solving the issues as they arose—not by shirking them—meeting them with wisdom, with the exercise of the most skilful and cautious judgment, but with fearless resolution when the time of crisis came.

He met each crisis on its own merits; he never sought excuse for shirking a task in the fact that it was different from the one he had expected to face. The long public career, which opened when as a boy he carried a musket in the ranks and closed when as a man in the prime of his intellectual strength he stood among the world's chief statesmen, came to what it was because he treated each triumph as opening the road to fresh effort, not as an excuse for ceasing from effort.

He undertook mighty tasks. Some of them he finished completely; others we must finish; and there remain yet others which he did not have to face, but which, if we are worthy to be the inheritors of his principles, we will in our turn face with the same resolution, the same sanity, the same unfaltering belief in the greatness of this country, and unfaltering championship of the rights of each and all of our people, which marked his high and splendid career.

THE LAW CAN DO SOME-THING, BUT THE LAW NEVER YET MADE A FOOL WISE OR A COW-ARD BRAVE OR A WEAKLING STRONG. ❧ ❧

# Strenuous Epigrams

Now at the outset of the century we are facing difficult and complex problems, problems social and economical, which will tax the best energies of all of us to solve right, and which we can only solve at all if we approach them in a spirit not merely of common sense, but of generous desire to act each for all and all for each.

When you take up science, art, and literature, remember that one first-class bit of work is better than one thousand fairly good bits of work; that as the years roll on, the man or the woman who has been able to make a masterpiece with the pen, the brush, the pencil, in any way, that that man, that woman, has rendered a service to the country such as not all his or her compeers who merely do fairly good second-rate work can ever accomplish.

In the long run, the most unpleasant truth is a safer companion than a pleasant falsehood.

The man or woman who seeks to bring up children to secure happiness by avoiding trouble; to bring them up so they cannot stand tough knocks, is wronging the children in a way and a degree that no other human being could wrong them. If you want your children to be successful you should teach them that the life that is worth living is worth working for. What a wretched life is that of a man who seeks to shirk the burden laid on us in this world! It is equally ignoble in either case, whether it is a man of wealth or one who earns his bread by the sweat of his brow.

The greatness of the fathers becomes to the children a shameful thing if they use it only as an excuse for inaction instead of as a spur to effort for noble aims.

All the time, gentlemen, we have people—often entirely well meaning—who will rise up and tell us that by some patent device we can all be saved in citizenship or in social life. Now, general, and you, and you who wear the button, when you came down to the root of things in war time you had to depend upon the qualities of manhood which had made good soldiers from the days when the children of Israel marched out of Egypt down.

Rifles now, instead of bows then, but the man behind the rifle is more important than the rifle is itself.

Now the great problem that we should set before us is to keep prosperity, to render its advantages less unequal, to try to secure a greater equality of its benefits, but above all, never under any circumstances to lend ourselves to the leadership of any who appeal to the baser passions of mankind, and who, because there is inequality in prosperity, would seek to substitute for that unequal prosperity community in disaster.

Remember that always. Evils have come through our very prosperity, but in warring against evil let us be exceeding careful not to war against the prosperity. As I have said before today once, it is mighty easy to destroy any disease if you are willing to kill the patient, but it is not good for the patient.

Let us face the fact that there are evils. It is foolish to blink at those evils. Let us set ourselves, but temperately and with sanity, to strive to find out what the evils are and to remedy them.

Brilliancy is a good thing. So is genius. But normally what we want is not genius, but the faculty of seeing that we know how to apply the copy-book moralities that we write down, and as long as we think of them only as fit for the copy-book there is not much use in us.

It is a very good thing, indeed, it is an indispensable thing, to have material well-being. You have got to have that at the base of our civilization, but if you do not build something more on top of it you have only got the foundation, and the foundation is a mighty bad place in which to live. It is essential to have it and you have got to have it for the support of the superstructure, but you have got to have the superstructure put in in addition to the material prosperity.

Poverty is a bitter thing, but it is not as bitter as restless vacuity and physical, moral, and intellectual flabbiness to which those doom themselves who elect to spend all their years in that vainest of all vain pursuits—pursuit of mere pleasure as a sufficient end in itself.

You are not going to do very much good with human nature if you attempt to take the bad out of it, by leaving a vacuum, for that vacuum is going to be filled with something, and if you do not fill it with what is good it will be filled with what is evil.

We must have honest, fearless, and able administration, the enforcement of law, but the law must be so framed and so administered as to secure justice for all alike—a square deal for every man, great or small, rich or poor.

That we have got to have. It will then still remain true that the chief factor in any man's individual success must be the sum of those qualities which we speak of as character in any man—his energy, his perseverance, his intelligence, his business thrift; no laws, however good, could begin to supply the lack of those qualities in any man.

Prosperity by itself never made any man happy.

The old pioneer days are gone, with their roughness and their hardship, their incredible toil and their wild half-savage romance. But the need for the pioneer virtues remains the same as ever.

The peculiar frontier conditions have vanished, but the manliness and stalwart hardihood of the frontiersmen can be given even freer scope under the conditions surrounding the complex industrialism of the present day.

We must insist upon courage and resolution, upon hardihood, tenacity and fertility in resource; we must insist upon the strong virile virtues, and we must insist no less upon the virtues of self-restraint, self-mastery, regard for the rights of others; we must show our abhorrence of cruelty, brutality, and corruption, in public and in private life alike.

You have got to have morality first, but if morality has not common sense with it, the result is apt to be unhappy.

The law can do something, but the law never yet made a fool wise or a coward brave or a weakling strong.

If the man has not got in him the stuff out of which he can work success, the state cannot supply it. What can be done by the state, by the nation, is to make the conditions such that each man shall be able under the best circumstances, with everything most favourable to him, to work out his fate for himself.

If under those circumstances he fails, I am sorry for him. I will help him as far as possible. I will lift him up if he stumbles but I won't try to carry him, for that is neither healthy for him nor for me.

If you don't know how to handle your gun, you will be beaten by a man with a club.

Education is not enough. The men of thin intellects, the men who are only competent to feel intellectual emotion, are not the men who will make a great nation. You have got to have in addition to the intellect what counts for much more than that—character. And in character you have got to have men good, and you have got to have them strong.

In private life there are few things more obnoxious than the man who is always loudly boasting, and if the boaster is not prepared to back up his words his position becomes absolutely contemptible. So it is with the nation.

Before we can do anything with the higher life, before we can have the higher thinking, there must be enough of material comfort to allow for at least plain living. We have got to have that first before we can do the high thinking; but if we are to count in the long run, we must have built upon the material prosperity the power and desire to give to our lives other than a merely material side.

If there is one lesson which I think each of us learns as he grows older, it is that it is not what the man works at, provided, of course, it is respectable and honourable in character, that fixes his place; it is the way he works at it.

A NATION MUST FIRST TAKE CARE TO DO WELL ITS DUTIES WITHIN ITS OWN BORDERS, BUT MUST NOT MAKE OF THAT FACT AN EXCUSE FOR FAILING TO DO THOSE OF ITS DUTIES THE PERFORMANCE OF WHICH LIE WITHOUT ITS OWN BORDERS. ❧ ❧

❧    ❧    ❧

Envy is merely the meanest form of admiration, and a man who envies another admits thereby his own inferiority.

Now when we come to the question of good citizenship, the first requisite is that a man shall do the homely, every-day humdrum duties well. A man is not a good citizen, I do not care how lofty his thoughts are about citizenship in the abstract, if in the concrete his actions do not bear them out, and it does not make much difference how high are his aspirations for mankind at large if he does not behave well in his own family, those aspirations are not going to bear very visible fruit.

He has got to be a good breadwinner, he has got to take care of his wife and children, he has got to be a neighbour whom his neighbours can trust. He has got to act squarely in his business relations—he has got to do all those every-day and ordinary things first or he is not a good citizen.

He has got to do more than that. In this country of ours he has got to devote, the average citizen has got to devote, a good deal of thought and time to the affairs of the state as a whole or those affairs are going to go badly, and he has got to devote that thought and that time steadily and intelligently.

❦   ❦   ❦

A nation must first take care to do well its duties within its own borders, but must not make of that fact an excuse for failing to do those of its duties the performance of which lie without its own borders.

❦   ❦   ❦

Publicity itself would cure many evils. The light of day is a great deterrent to wrong-doing. If the mere fact of being able to put it nakedly and with the certainty that the statements were true a given condition of things that was wrong would go a long distance toward curing that wrong.

It is easy for those who stay at home in comfort, who never have to see humanity in the raw, or to strive against the dreadful naked forces which appear clothed, hidden and subdued in civilized life—it is easy for such to criticize the men who, in rough fashion, and amid grim surroundings, make ready the way for the higher life that is to come afterward; but let us all remember that the untempted and the effortless should be cautious in passing too heavy judgment upon their brethren who may show hardness, who may be guilty of shortcomings, but who nevertheless do the great deeds by which mankind advances.

It is not enough to have mere aspiration after righteousness; it is not enough to have the lofty ideal; with it must go the power of in some sort practically realizing it.

I do not care whether a man is a banker or a bricklayer; if he is a good banker or a good bricklayer he is a good citizen; if he is dishonest, if he is tricky, if he shirks his job or tries to cheat his neighbour, be he great or small, be he the poor man cheating the rich man, or the rich man oppressing the poor man, in either case he is a bad citizen.

I see everywhere I stop—in Maine, as in Massachusetts, New Hampshire, and Connecticut—men who, in the times that tried the nation's worth, rose level to the nation's need, and offered up life gladly upon the nation's altar—the men who fought in the great Civil War from '61 to '65.

They taught us much by their life in war time, and they have taught us as much by their life ever since.

They were soldiers when we needed soldiers, and they were of the very best kind, and when the need was for citizenship in civil life they showed us they could give the highest kind of citizenship. Not merely did they give us a reunited country;

not merely did they leave us the memory of the great deeds they did to be for ever after an inspiration to us, but they left us the memory of the way the deed was done.

Let us resolutely refuse to use the knife that will be less dangerous for the disease than the sufferer.

While I hope that as the chance occurs each man will get all the fun he can out of life, remember that when it comes not merely to looking back upon it, but to living it, the kind of life that is worth living is the kind of life that is embodied in duty worth doing which is well done.

Nothing can make good citizenship in men who have not got in them courage, hardihood, decency, sanity, the spirit of truth-telling and truth-seeking, the spirit that dares and endures, the spirit that knows what it is to have a lofty ideal, and yet to endeavour to realize that ideal in practical fashion.

Sometimes each of us has the feeling that if he has to choose between the fool and the knave he will take the knave, because he can reform him perhaps, and he cannot reform the fool; and even hardness of heart is not much more destructive in the long run than softness of head.

The abler a man is in his business, in politics, in social leadership, the worse he is if he is a scoundrel, whether his scoundrelism takes the form of corruption in business, corruption in politics, or that most sinister of all forms, the effort to rise by inciting class hatred, by inciting lawlessness, by exciting the spirit of evil, the spirit of jealousy and envy as between man and man.

The man who makes up for ten days' indifference to duty by an eleven-days' morbid repentance about that indifference is of scant use in the world.

We need strong bodies. More than that we need strong minds, and finally we need what counts for more than body, for more than mind—character—character, into which many elements enter, but three above all. In the first place, morality, decency, clean living, the faculty of treating fairly those around about, the qualities that make a man a decent husband, a decent father, a good neighbour, a good man to deal with or to work beside; the quality that makes a man a good citizen of the state, careful to wrong no one; we need that first as the foundation, and if we have not got that, no amount of strength or courage or ability can take its place. No matter how able a man is, how good a soldier naturally, if the man were a traitor, then the abler he was the more dangerous he was to the regiment, to the army, to the nation. It is so in business, in politics, in every relation of life. The abler a man is, if he is a corrupt politician, an unscrupulous business man, a demagogic agitator who seeks to set one portion of his fellow men against the other, his ability makes him but by so much more a curse to the community at large. In character we must have virtue, morality, decency, square dealing as the foundation; and it is not enough. It is only the foundation. In war you needed to have the man decent, patriotic, but no matter how patriotic he was, if he ran away he was no good. So it is in citizenship; the virtue that stays at home in its own parlour and bemoans the wickedness of the outside world is of scant use to the community.

We are a vigorous, masterful people, and the man who is to do good work in our country must not only be a good man, but also emphatically a man. We must have the qualities of courage, of hardihood, of power to hold one's own in the hurly burly of actual life. We must have the manhood that shows on fought fields and that shows in the work of the business world and in the struggles of civic life. We must have manliness, courage, strength, resolution, joined to decency and morality, or we shall make but poor work of it. Finally, those two qualities by themselves are not enough. In addition to decency, and courage, we must have the saving grace of common sense. We all of us have known decent and valiant fools who have meant so well that it made it all the more pathetic that the effect of their actions was so ill.

In this country we have room for every honest man who spends his life in honest effort; we have no room either for the man of means who, in a spirit of arrogant baseness, looks down upon the man less well off, or for the other man who envies his neighbour because that neighbour happens to be better off. Either feeling is a base feeling, unworthy of a self-respecting man.

❧   ❧   ❧

Every man of us needs help, needs more and more to be given the chance to show forth in himself the stuff that is in him, and this kind of free library is doing in the world of cultivation, the world of civilization, what it should or may do for the great world of political and social development; that is, it is, as far as may be, equalizing the opportunities and then leaving the men themselves to show how able they are to take advantage of those opportunities.

❧   ❧   ❧

If you use envy in the ordinary sense of the word, its existence implies a feeling of inferiority in the man who feels it, a feeling that a self-respecting man will be ashamed to have.

❧   ❧   ❧

In our life what we need is not so much genius, not so much brilliancy as the ordinary common place every-day qualities which a man needs in private life, and which he needs just as much in public life.

It is rare, indeed, that a great work, a work supremely worth doing, can be done save at the cost not only of labour and toil, but of much puzzling worry during the time of the performance.

Any generation fit to do its work must work for the future, for the people of the future, as well as for itself.

Mankind goes ahead but slowly, and it goes ahead mainly through each of us trying to do, or at least through each of the majority of us trying to do, the best that is in him, and to do it in the most intelligent and sanest way.

We have founded our republic on the theory that the average man will as a rule do the right thing, that in the long run the majority is going to decide by what is sane and wholesome.

If our fathers were mistaken in that theory, if through events becoming such that not occasionally but persistently the mass of the people do what is unwholesome, what is wrong, then the republic cannot stand, I care not how good its laws, I care not in what marvellous mechanism its constitution may be embodied.

Back of the laws, back of the administration, back of our system of government lies the man, lies the average manhood of our people, and in the long run we are going to go up or are going to go down, accordingly as the average standard of our citizenship does or does not wax in growth and grace.

Neither you nor any one else can make a man wise or cultivate him. All you can do is to give him a chance to make himself, to add to his own wisdom or his own cultivation, and that is all you can do in any kind of genuine philanthropic work. The only philanthropic work is work that helps a man to help himself. This is true in every way, socially and sociologically. The man who will submit or demand to be carried is not worth carrying.

It is a good thing to be a good half-back, but it is a mighty bad thing if at forty all you can say of a man is that he was a good half-back.

ANY GENER-
ATION FIT
TO DO ITS WORK
MUST WORK FOR
THE FUTURE,
FOR THE PEOPLE
OF THE FUTURE,
AS WELL AS FOR
ITSELF. ❧ ❧

Exactly as infinitely the happiest woman is she who has born and brought up many healthy children, so infinitely the happiest man is he who has toiled hard and successfully in his life-work.

There are two attributes of which as a people we need to beware more than of any others—the arrogance which looks down on those not so well off, and treats them with brutal and selfish disregard for their interests, and the equally base spirit of hatred and rancour for those that are better off.

If you haven't got it in you to feel most proud of the times when you work, I think very little of you.

The millennium is a good way off yet.

We cannot be dragged up, we have got to push ourselves up. No law that ever was devised can give wisdom to the fool, courage to the coward, strength to the weakling. We must have those qualities in us, for if they are not in us they cannot be gotten out of us.

I wish to sec the average American take in reference to his fellows the attitude that I wish to see America take among the nations of the world: the attitude of one who scorns equally to flinch from injustice by the strong and to do injustice to the weak.

You fought for liberty under the law, not liberty in spite of the law. Any man who claims that there can be liberty in spite of and against the law is claiming that anarchy is liberty. From the beginning of time anarchy in all its forms has been the handmaiden, the harbinger, of despotism and tyranny.

Woe will beset this country if we draw lines of distinction between class and class, or creed and creed, or along any other line save that which divides good citizenship from bad citizenship.

I think that the average American is a decent fellow, and that the prime thing in getting him to get on well with the other average American is to have each remember that the other is a decent fellow, and try to look at the problems a little from the other's standpoint.

I would like to be President again, but I would far rather be a whole President for three years, than half a President for seven years. Remember that!

I would plead with my countrymen to show not any special brilliancy, or special genius, but the ordinary humdrum, commonplace qualities which, in the aggregate, spell success for the nation, and spell success for the individual.

Far more important, by far, than any question of mere political expediency or wisdom, is the question of our success as a nation of home-makers in the deepest and truest sense of the word.

If the average American home is such in fact as well as in name, if it contains plenty of healthy children, who are being brought up to be good citizens, we need have scant fear about the future.

❧    ❧    ❧

Courage and loyalty, the stern determination to do exact justice, the high purpose to struggle for the right, and the common sense to struggle for it in practical fashion—all these qualities we must show now, in our civil and social and business life, as you showed them when, in the days of your youth and lusty strength, you marched forth, an army with banners, and brought back the peace that comes, not to the weakling and the craven, but to those whose proud eyes tell of triumph tasted.

❧    ❧    ❧

To quote an expression that I am fond of, this sort of gift (a public library) is equally far from two prime vices of our civilization, hardness of heart, and softness of head.

❧    ❧    ❧

I believe, not in brilliancy, not in genius, I believe in the ordinary, humdrum, workaday virtues that make a man a good man in his family, a good neighbour, a good man to deal with in business, a good man to deal with in the state, and when you have got a man with those characteristics in him, you have a man who, if the need comes, will rise level to that need.

The well-being of the tiller of the soil and the wage-worker is the well-being of the state.

Get all the enjoyment you legitimately can out of life, but remember that the only sure way of getting, in the end, no enjoyment out of life, is to start in to make it the end of your existence.

It seems to me that the man has a right to call himself thrice blessed who has in him the combined power and purpose to use his wealth for the benefit of all the people at large, in a way that can do them real benefit, and in no way can more benefit be done, than through the gift of libraries, such as this.

No prosperity and no glory can save the nation that is rotten at heart. We must keep the core of our national being sound, and see to it that not only our citizens, but, above all, our statesmen in public life, practise the old, commonplace virtues which, from time immemorial, have lain at the root of all true national well-being.

Now it is of no possible use to decline to go through all the ordinary duties of citizenship for a long space of time, and then suddenly to get up and feel very angry about something or somebody, not clearly defined in one's mind, and demand reform, as if it was a concrete substance that could be handed out forthwith.

We must all either wear out or rust out, every one of us. My choice is to wear out.

The best institutions are no good if they won't work. I do not care how beautiful a theory is. If it won't fit in with the facts, it is no good. If you build the handsomest engine, and it won't go, its usefulness would be limited.

Every father and mother here, if they are wise, will bring up their children not to shirk difficulties, but to meet them, and overcome them, not to strive after a life of ignoble ease, but to strive to do their duty, first to themselves and their families, and then to the whole state, and this duty must inevitably take the shape of work in some form or other.

Our country has been populated by pioneers, and, therefore, it has in it more energy, more enterprise, more expansive power than any other in the world.

Remember that the chance to do the great heroic work may or may not come. If it does not come, then all that there can be to our credit is the faithful performance of every-day duty. That is all that most of us, throughout our lives, have the chance to do, and it is enough, because it is the beginning to do, because it means most for the nation when done, and if the time for the showing of heroism does come, you may guarantee that those who show it are most likely to be the people who have done their duty in average times, as the occasion for doing the duty arose.

I came from a college which boasts as its proudest building that which is to stand to the memory of Harvard's sons who responded to the call of Lincoln, when the hour of the nation's danger was at hand. It will be a bad day for this country, and a worse day for all educative institutions in this country, if ever such a call is made, and the men of college training do not feel it peculiarly incumbent upon them to respond.

We have but little room among our people for the timid, the irresolute, and the idle, and it is no less true that there is scant room in the world at large for the nation with mighty thews, that dares not to be great.

The poorest life that any one can live, from the standpoint of pleasure, is the life that has nothing but pleasure as its end and aim.

WE MUST ALL EITHER WEAR OUT OR RUST OUT EVERY ONE OF US. MY CHOICE IS TO WEAR OUT. ❧ ❧

It is not an easy thing to get a law that shall do us great benefit, but it is only too easy to get a law that shall do us great harm.

The abler, the more powerful any man is, the worse he is, if he has not got the root of righteousness in him.

The first thing that the individual man has to do is to pull his own weight, to earn his own way, not to be a drag on the community. And the individual who wants to do a tremendous amount in life, but who will not start by earning his own way in life, is not apt to be of much use in the world. He is akin to those admirable creatures who, from '61 to '65, were willing to begin as brigadier-generals. We must have first the desire to do well in the day of small things, the day through which all of us must pass, the day which lasts very long with most of us.

I do not care how moral a man is, and how brave he is, if he is a natural-born fool, you can do nothing with him. I ask, then, for decency as the foundation, for courage and manliness thereon, and finally, in addition to both, I ask for common sense as the moderator and guide of both.

Character has two sides. It is composed of two sets of traits; in the first place, the set of traits which we group together under such names as clean living, decency, morality, virtue, the desire and power to deal fairly each by his neighbour, each by his friends, each toward the state; that we have to have as fundamental. In addition, you must have hardihood, resolution, courage, the power to do, the power to dare, the power to endure, and when you have that combination, then you get the proper type of American citizenship.

The worth of a promise consists purely in the way in which the performance squares with it. That has got two sides to it. In the first place, if the man is an honest man, he will try just as hard to keep a promise made on the stump as one made off the stump. In the second place, if a people keep their heads, they will not wish promises to be made which are impossible of performance.

Sometimes we hear those who do not work spoken of with envy; surely the wilfully idle need arouse in the breast of a healthy man no emotion stronger than that of contempt—at the outside no emotion stronger than angry contempt.

I want to see a man take his own part. If he will not, his part is not worth taking. But, on the other hand, I have greatest contempt for a man who is always walking about wanting to pick a quarrel, or wanting to say something unpleasant about some one else.

The fact that he talks loud does not mean, necessarily, that he fights hard, either. Sometimes you see a man that will talk loud and fight hard, but he does not fight hard because he talks loud, but in spite of it.

Good, not harm, normally comes from the piling up of wealth through business enterprises. Probably the most serious harm resulting to us, the people of moderate means, is when we harm ourselves by letting the dark and evil vices of envy and hatred toward our fellows eat into our natures.

Now, in the navy you have got to have ships and good guns; but if you have not got anything else, the ships and the guns are worthless.

You have got to have a man behind the guns, the man in the engine-room. That is what counts; that is what made the difference at Manila and Santiago. There was a difference in the ships, too; but the great difference was in the men. And no kind of patent device on board any ship will take the place of cool, intelligent, and hardy courage in the officers and enlisted men.

So, exactly as you need in war the man behind the gun, you need in peace the man behind the plough, the man at the machine. It is on him that our success ultimately depends.

When you make it evident that no man shall be excused from violating the law, you make it evident that every man will be protected from violators of the law.

Remember that every man, at times, stumbles, and must be helped up; if he lies down you cannot carry him. He has got to be willing to walk. You can help him in but one way, the only way in which any man can be helped permanently—help him to help himself.

In the individual, nothing can take the place of his own qualities; in the community, nothing can take the place of the qualities of the average citizen.

Brilliancy, genius, cleverness of all kinds, do not count for anything like as much as the sturdy traits that we group together under the name of character.

The men who won in the Revolution, and made this country take its place among the nations of the earth, did it because they had in them courage, resolution, integrity, unbending will, and common sense.

❧        ❧        ❧

Abraham Lincoln—the spirit incarnate of those who won victory in the Civil War—was the true representative of this people, not only for his own generation, but for all time, because he was a man among men, a man who embodied the qualities of his fellow men, but who embodied them to the highest, and the most unusual degree of perfection, who embodied all that there was in the nation of courage, of wisdom, of gentle, patient kindliness, and of common sense.

And great, sad, patient Lincoln led us to victory from '61 to '65 because he did not trust to any mere trick or device, because he drove deep down to the heart of thousands, and based his reliance on the fundamental virtues of mankind—the old, old virtues of mankind.

That is the spirit we have to show in facing the problems of today. If we approach those problems in a spirit of hysteria, we will fail, as we well deserve to fail; if we approach them in a spirit of envy and rancour and malice toward our fellows, we will not only fail, but we will drag them and us in a common ruin.

Shame to us if we blink the evils! They are there. Shame to us if we fear to face the problem! It is there, and to say that it is not there will not prove its absence.

Face the problem; realize its gravity, and then approach it in a spirit, not merely of determination to solve it, but of hearty desire to solve it with justice to all, with malice to none; to solve it in a spirit of broad kindliness and charity, in a spirit that will keep us ever in mind that if we are to succeed at all, it must be by each doing, to the best of his capacity, his own business, and yet by each remembering that in a sense he is also his brother's keeper.

Success comes only to those who lead the life of endeavour. The man who works, the man who does great deeds, in the end dies, as surely as the veriest idler who cumbers the earth's surface, but he leaves behind him the great fact that he has done his work well.

The able, fearless, unscrupulous man, who is not guided by the law, is a curse, to be hunted down like a civic wild beast, and his ability and his courage, whether in business, in politics, or anywhere else, only serve to make him more dangerous and a greater curse.

Timid people, people scant of faith and hope, and good people, who are not accustomed to the roughness of the life of effort, are almost sure to be disheartened and dismayed by the work and the worry, and overmuch cast down by the shortcomings, actual or seeming, which, in real life, always accompany the first stages even of what eventually turn out to be the most brilliant victories.

I want to see the average American citizen be in the future, as he has been in the past, a decent man, doing no wrong, and, on the other hand, able to hold his own also.

If there is any one quality which is not admirable, whether in a nation or in an individual, it is hysterics, either in religion or in anything else.

I would teach the young men that he who has not wealth owes his first duty to his family, while he who has means owes his to the state. It is ignoble to go on heaping money on money. I would preach the doctrine of work to all, and to men of wealth the doctrine of unremunerative work.

I do not believe in a bluff. I feel about a nation as we all feel about a man; let him not say anything that he cannot make good, and having said it, let him make it good.

It is pleasant to learn by an experience which teaches us what to follow instead of what to avoid.

When I address an audience like this, which takes part itself in all the workings of the government, I do not have to explain, as I have to explain to some other audiences, that the government cannot do everything.

You can do a good deal through the town, but you can do a great deal more for the town than the town can do for you. And some of our people make the mistake of thinking you can work that, but you cannot.

We need in our public life, as in our private life, the virtues that every one could practise if he would. We need the will to practise them. There are two kinds of greatness that can be achieved. There is the greatness that comes to the man who can do what no one else can do. That is a mighty rare kind, and, of course, it can only be achieved by the man of special and unusual qualities.

Then there is the other kind that comes to the man who does the things that every one could do, but that every one does not do. Who goes ahead and does them himself. To do that, you first of all have got to school yourself to do the ordinary, commonplace things.

❧     ❧     ❧

There has never yet been a man in our history who led a life of ease whose name is worth remembering.

Now, understand me. Take holidays. I believe in holidays. I believe in play, and I believe in playing hard while you play, but don't make a business of it.

Do your work, and do it up to the handle, and then play when you have got time to play, and, if you are worth anything, enjoy that too.

❧     ❧     ❧

Now what is true of the individual is true of the nation. The heroic times in this nation's

IT IS A GOOD THING TO BE A GOOD HALFBACK, BUT IT IS A MIGHTY BAD THING IF AT FORTY ALL YOU CAN SAY OF A MAN IS THAT HE WAS A GOOD HALFBACK.

career were when it had great work to do, and, instead of flinching from the work, did it, and it did that heroic work in part because, at the hour of need, it showed it possessed heroic virtues, the heroic virtues that a great and generous nation must show and will show in the crises of its history; and also because, in addition to the heroic virtues, which can be used but once in a generation, it had those commonplace, humdrum, every-day virtues which save us year in and year out, and if we do not have those virtues, if we do not have those qualities, you can guarantee that when the hour calls for heroism we won't have that either.

There is need to do all the ordinary, commonplace duties as they arise, or we will be in no shape to meet the crisis that calls for heroism when that crisis arises.

Now you, representatives of the great war, who are here today, when you went out from '61 to '65, the men by whose sides you fought had to have certain traits.

No one trait was enough. They had to be patriotic in the first place. They had to be driven onward by a love for country that made them willing to spend the best years of their youth and early manhood in the service of the nation to their own detriment; that made them willing to stake all life itself for the great prize of death in battle, for the honour of the flag. You had to have that spirit first.

You had to have more than that. I do not care how patriotic a man was, if he had a tendency to run away he was no good. Besides the love of country you had to have, to make a good soldier, a strong, virile purpose in the man, eagerness to do his work as a man. He had to have courage, strength, fixity of resolution.

It was not all victory. You met defeats, and the man who after defeat thought he would go home was of no use. You had to have the man who after defeat would come up and try again, and if he was defeated again, come up and try again until he wrested from defeat the splendid ultimate triumph. The men who are going to do good work for citizenship in this community are the men who approach its duties in the spirit, sirs, that you approached yours in the time of the Civil War, who are not going to expect everything to be done for them, but who are going to do their share of it; who are not going to expect the way to be easy and smooth, for the path of national greatness never is easy or smooth, but who are going to face the rough work of the world with the determination to do that work aright.

A government can do something; it can do a good deal; but it can never begin to do as much for the individual as the individual can do for the government.

I think there is only one quality worse than hardness of heart, and that is softness of head.

Now let each man here look back in his life and think what it is that he is proud of in it—what part of it he is glad to hand on as a memory to his sons and daughters.

Is it his hours of ease? No, not a bit. It is the memory of his success, of his triumph, and the triumph and the success could only come through effort.

Is that not true? Let each one think for himself. Look back in your career, and if you have not got it in you to feel most proud of the time when you worked, I think but little of you.

In this life, as a rule, the job that is easy to do is not very well worth while doing.

In life what counts as the chief factor in the success of a man or a woman is character, and character is partly inborn and partly developed; partly developed by the man's individual will, the woman's individual will, partly developed by the wise training of those above the young man or young woman, the boy or the girl, partly developed by the myriad associations of life.

Speaking broadly, prosperity must, of necessity, come to all of us or to none of us; of course there are sporadic exceptions, individual and local.

It is, in the long run, the man that counts. Just exactly as in war, though you have got to have the best weapons, yet they are useless if the men behind them don't handle them well; so in peace, the best constitution, the best legislation, the greatest natural advantages will avail nothing if you have not the right type of citizenship to take advantage of them.

Above all, gentlemen, let us remember that bad laws and bad administration can completely nullify all efforts for good upon the part of the private citizen.

About all we have a right to expect from government is that it will see that the cards are not stacked, and if it sees to that, then we will abide by the deal.

Every one who thinks, knows that the only way in which any problem of great importance was ever successfully solved was by constant and persistent effort toward a given end—effort that did not end with any one election or with any one year, but that was continued steadily, temperately, but resolutely, toward a given end.

Strength of any kind, physical, mental, is but a source of danger if it is not guided aright. On the other hand, it is just as important for every man or woman, who is striving for decency, to keep ever in mind the further fact that unless there is power, efficiency, behind the effort for decency, scant is the good that will come.

Good fortune does not come only to the good, nor bad fortune only to the unjust. When the weather is good for crops it is also good for weeds; moreover, not only do the wicked flourish, when the times are such that most men flourish, but what is worse, the spirit of envy and jealousy and hatred springs up in the breasts of those who, though they may be doing fairly well themselves, yet see others, who are no more deserving, doing far better.

Normally, the nation that achieves greatness, like the individual who achieves greatness, can do so only at the cost of anxiety and bewilderment and heart-wearing effort.

It is a good thing for a nation to demand in its representatives intellect, but it is a better thing to demand in them that sum of qualities which we talk of as character.

If you are dealing with a man in a business way, whether as employer or employee, or in commerce with a storekeeper, or with any one, you want him to be a smart man, but it is a mighty bad thing if he is only smart.

I would not preach to any man the life of ease, the life of safety only. Instead of the life of ease I preach, to all worthy to be called men, the life of work, the life of endeavour, and instead of the life of safety I preach the doctrine that teaches us now, as it taught the men of the Civil War, that there are times when safety is the last thing to be considered.

A free library, where each man, each woman, has the chance to get for himself or herself the training that he has the character to desire and to acquire. Now, of course, our common school system lies at the foundation of our educational system, but it is the foundation only. The men that are to stand preeminent as the representatives of the culture of the community must educate themselves.

I pity no man because he has to work. If he is worth his salt, he will work. I envy the man who has a work worth doing and does it well.

You can pardon most anything in a man who will tell the truth, because you know where that man is; you know what he means. If any one lies, if he has the habit of untruthfulness, you cannot deal with him, because there is nothing to depend on. You cannot tell what can be done with him or by his aid. Truth-telling is a virtue upon which we should not only insist in the schools and at home, but in business and in politics just as much. The business man or politician who does not tell the truth, cheats; and for the cheat we should have no use in any walk of life.

About the worst quality you can have in a soldier is hysterics, or anything approaching it, and it is pretty nearly the worst quality in civil life. We need in civil life the plain, practical, every-day virtues, which all of us admit in theory to be necessary, and when we all practise them we will come mighty near making a state perfect.

The man who has not got great tasks to do cannot achieve greatness. Greatness only comes because the task to be done is great. The men who lead lives of mere ease, of mere pleasure, the men who go through life seeking how to avoid trouble, to avoid risk, to avoid effort, to them it is not given to achieve greatness. Greatness comes only

WOE WILL BESET THIS COUNTRY IF WE DRAW LINES OF DISTINCTION BETWEEN CLASS AND CLASS, OR CREED AND CREED, OR ALONG ANY OTHER LINE SAVE THAT WHICH DIVIDES GOOD CITIZENSHIP FROM BAD CITIZEN-SHIP. ॐ ॐ ॐ ॐ

to those who seek not how to avoid obstacles, but how to overcome them.

I believe in work, and I believe in play. I would be sorry not to see you enjoy yourselves, but do not let play interfere with work. Do things quietly and carefully. Boys, remember the manlier you wish to be, the nicer you can afford to be at home. I would be ashamed of a boy who was a bully to the weak. When you play, be fair, but play hard, and then work hard at your studies. If you get hurt, keep on playing. Work with your whole heart in all things.

There never has been devised, and there never will be devised, any law which will enable a man to succeed save by the exercise of those qualities which have always been the prerequisites of success, the qualities of hard work, of keen intelligence, of unflinching will.

Laws are good things, but they are only the implements with which the men who make them, and live under them, work out their own salvation and the salvation of the nation.

Each man must work for himself. If he cannot support himself, he will be but a drag on all mankind, but each man must work for the common good. There is not a man here who does not, at times, need to have a helping hand extended to him, and shame on the brother who will not extend that helping hand.

The citizen that counts, the man that counts in our life is the man who endeavours not to shirk difficulties, but to meet and overcome them; is the man who endeavours not to lead his life in the world's soft places, not to walk easily and take his comfort; but the man who goes out to tread the rugged ways that lead to honour and success, the ways, the treading of which means good work worthily done.

It is a good lesson for nations and individuals to learn never to hit if it can be helped, and never to hit soft.

I ask, then, that all of us approach our duties of today in the spirit that our fathers have shown in the different crises of the past, that we approach them, realizing that nothing can take the place of the ordinary, every-day performance of duty, that we need the virtues which do not wait for heroic times, but which are exercised day in and day out in the ordinary work, the ordinary duty of the life domestic, the life social, the life in reference to the State; and if we show those qualities, if we show the qualities that make for good citizenship, for decency and civic righteousness in ordinary times, my faith is firm that when the need for the heroic efforts arises, our people will, in the future, as they have always done in the past, show that they have the capacity for heroic work.